ISBN 911868-33-X

CASS SCENIC
OF WES

by Frederick A. Kramer
photography by John Krause

RAIL-CRAFT

C33

LIBRARY

FRONT COVER: Cass Scenic Railway No. 5 presents a mood of a bygone era in the verdant hills of West Virginia. The Cass roster includes more than a fair share of geared steam locomotives. Kodachrome by Jim Boyd was shot on a Railfan Weekend.

OPPOSITE PAGE: The Cass is a natural for spectacular flash photos at night, such as this view of No. 7 taking water. Jim Boyd set camera on tripod, shutter open, with multiple flashes to suit his idea of a great railroad photo.

BELOW: Steam locomotives require constant maintenance and the Cass treats her power with great care. Original Mower Lumber Company shops in rear served Cass also until destroyed in fire. Modern shops have been rebuilt on the original site. Jim Boyd photo.

Carstens
PUBLICATIONS, INC.

Fredon-Springdale Road
Fredon, New Jersey

Address all mail to:
P.O. Box 700, Newton, New Jersey 07860

PREFACE

HIGH UPON Cheat Mountain and back across the crests, a soaring wave of giant spruce once ruled the endless skyline. It was virgin forest, immense and inaccessible. The courage, sweat, and stamina of more than half a century would be needed for men to harvest this towering woodland wealth.

Central to the ambitious undertaking was the means for bringing the trees down from their mountain stand. A logging railroad was needed, not built to ordinary standards, but shaped to conform to the steepness and sharp turns of the land. The locomotives could not be ordinary either, for these hills demanded the sure-footed traction that only a gear-driven design can provide.

What was it like up there on the mountain, shoved headlong toward the clouds on a logging car? And can we get a feel for the lumberjacks' domain, that dramatic realm so prominent in West Virginia's history?

One sure way to find out is to ride the Cass Scenic Railroad. In these pages, that trip is recorded in a blend of logging history and touring scenes. In here is Cass, busy with saw logs being shunted to the mill, smoky preparations in the shop area along Leatherbark Creek, the scurry up the mountain to the log landing, and finally, the transition from lumber days to the operations that make the Cass Scenic Railroad unique.

You'll see pictures of railroaders and lumbermen at work. There are those who witnessed all the changes, such as Harry Gum whose family farm was here before there was a Cass. There were many others, of course, whose patient striving has made the changes and heritage of Cass worth preserving. Few gave more of themselves to nurture that once-frail dream than the late Kyle Neighbors. To him, and to his many friends who helped, this pictorial review is respectfully dedicated.

Double heading downgrade, a train of observation cars returns
from the mountain heights. The cloud shadows, clearings, and a
smoky veil casade across the hills proclaiming this majesty: it is
West Virginia.

CASS
—the town and the man.

THE TOWN OF CASS really isn't very old. By-passed by the westward wave of farmers, this rugged area remained a frontier even as the twentieth century approached.

In the two decades that preceded the turn of the century, the sawmill industry had come of age. Steam power and band saws had given the mills a voracious appetite for logs in continuous, prodigious amounts. These developments and the adaptation of railroads to logging purposes suddenly gave a different economic perspective to remote, forested hill country.

It was this Industrial Age turning point that extended the scope of Sam Slaymaker's thoughts. Slaymaker had been lumbering in the Greenbrier Valley, concentrating on the best specimens of white pine. Their premium value justified the expense of manual labor and the hazards of rafting his logs down the river to market. Slaymaker had been climbing around the hills too, looking for prime timber. He found the superb, immense stand of red spruce atop Cheat Mountain.

The Chesapeake & Ohio Railroad proceeded with their plan to build the Greenbrier branch, straight into this area so rich with natural resources. For Slaymaker, that action was the essential key. He formed his own company, bought 173,000 acres of excellent timberland, and started to work.

The construction camp went up in 1900, right where Cass stands today. From this camp, the logging railroad was built up onto Cheat Mountain and over to the headwaters of the Elk River. Appropriately named the Greenbrier & Elk River Railroad, it was the original ancestor of the Cass Scenic Railroad we ride today.

The substantial investments needed for the railroad, the mill, camps, and supplies eventually exceeded Slaymaker's ability to finance them by himself. By 1902, he found himself a part owner of the West Virginia Spruce Lumber Company. And on Washington's birthday, that year of 1902, the mill at Cass was started. The boom was underway.

Spruce is a light wood, moderately strong and well-suited for general construction. Although it is not a premium wood, much of the timber not suitable as saw logs is excellent as pulpwood for making paper.

For a spruce cutting operation to be profitable, it was necessary to have a regular customer for the pulpwood that would account for nearly half of the total volume. The market for the pulpwood was a narrow one, quite unlike the wide, general market for lumber from the sawmill. West Virginia Spruce Lumber was fortunate to find and contract with the West Virginia Pulp & Paper Company to take their pulpwood.

West Virginia Pulp & Paper was a name that went back into the 1880's. However, by the time Slaymaker was looking for someone to buy his pulpwood, the name had been bought up and re-established by an enterprising pair of men in the paper business from Altoona, Pennsylvania. One of these men was a fifty-two year older named Joseph Kerr Cass.

Cass was a driving force. He spent his first eight years out of college surveying for the Grand Rapids & Indiana Railway and then formed a partnership in the paper business. By 1899, Cass had over two decades of experience in the paper industry and it was then that he helped form the modern-day West Virginia Pulp & Paper Company, using the old company's name and his own partnership as the base.

Joseph Cass was both vice president and one of the directors of the pulp company when Slaymaker was negotiating for the sale of his pulpwood. When the townsite was named Cass, a well-placed honor had been bestowed, for Cass went on to become chairman of the board in 1909. In that same year, West Virginia Spruce Lumber Company was merged into West Virginia Pulp & Paper. Cass lived to be 90, not passing on until 1938 by which time he had

This wooden frame depot once stood at Cass. Belonging to the
Chesapeake & Ohio Railroad, it greeted the daily passenger and
mail train that served their Greenbrier Division from the mainline at Ronceverte, 84 miles away. The drama of this nighttime
activity was captured during a weekend excursion conducted
for a group of railfans. Fire, that perennial tormentor of lumber
towns, claimed the depot and ended matters for this traditional
symbol of Cass hospitality.

Michael Koch collection

The original sawmill at Cass is seen above when it was less than three years old. Trains were unloaded at the right by spilling the logs into the pond. Closely contained there until selected for sawing, the logs were then hauled up the jack slip and onto the log deck where the band saws were located. This mill burned in 1922 and was replaced by the mill below, seen from the opposite end. Capable of cutting 250,000 feet of lumber a day, the new mill was truly large and doubled the cutting capacity at Cass. The plant was powered by steam that was generated by burning sawdust and trimmings, thus requiring a spark arrester on the smokestack.

Pocahontas Supply Company, a West Virginia Pulp & Paper subsidiary, operated the company stores. At Cass, the store and offices were in the white building in the background. A box car is being spotted at the receiving platform by using a string of empty log cars to push it into position. This kept the weight of the engine off the little coal dock in the foreground. The darker tone building would one day become Kyle Neighbors' museum.

seen his company manage to pay dividends throughout the Depression's most difficult years.

Cass, the town, was a product of its times. It was a boomtown with boardwalks that kept people out of the mud and a company store run in the classic manner. The only reason for living in Cass was to have a close relationship with the lumber operation. The total population could be said to be 2000, but that counted the men who lived up in the hills in the logging camps. The townsfolk were mill workers, the railroad men, a few clerks and clerics.

On Saturday nights, Cass was a different town. The men who had worked so hard during the week came down from camp ready to let off steam. The homeguard really didn't care for the brawling insobriety and matters finally settled down by confining the Saturday night crowd to an area across the river. That was outside of town. Then, after all the red-eye had been consumed, the roistering and red-lighting done, it was up into the hills some more.

The pride of any mill town is its mill, and Cass was no exception. Located north of town, it has been unused since 1960. Actually, we now look at the second mill, the first one having burned in 1922. Fire was the number one enemy of sawmills, for very few were built with masonry and all were filled with combustible sawdust and trimmings. When the Cass mill was rebuilt, its size and capacity were doubled.

Sawmilling is a manufacturing process, essentially a production line that converts saw logs into graded, commercial size lumber. From the log trains, the logs were dumped into a mill pond where they could be collected, cleaned, and readily handled when it came time to feed them into the mill.

Logs entered the mill by the jack slip, a V-shaped ramp with a power-driven chain that had hooks on it to catch the logs. The logs were thus dragged up the ramp and disengaged onto a log deck inside the mill where they were queued up for sawing. Steam powered machinery released the logs one at a time onto a carriage and rotated the log on the carriage until the best surface was ready for the first cut. The log was then firmly gripped by a mechanism on the carriage and fed slowly into the band saw. Because the mill was a noisy place, the sawyer controlled positioning and thickness of cut by means of handsignals to the setter who rode the carriage.

Generally, band saws produced thick planks, slabs, and square timbers. Smaller sizes were produced by using resaws. The product was further trimmed and edged to standard dimension. Finally, the pieces were graded and stacked by hand in the drying yard before being shipped out. At Cass, the drying yards extended from the mill toward the depot, occupying the present parking lot area.

Sawmilling is skilled and dangerous work, but the pitched whine of the saws, the motion of machinery at work, and above all, the aroma of freshly sawn lumber lend a heady atmosphere. A working sawmill can never be forgotten, seeming somehow to leave a little sawdust in the veins of the beholder.

Having backed down toward the depot, a log train now clears
the switch in back of the camera and starts forward toward the
mill. The landmarks of Cass are seen in the background and the
stacks of lumber crowding the side track at the left are in the
process of air-drying. [OPPOSITE:] When a log train entered the
mill siding, it stopped traffic on the C&O's branch line. The
engine is just entering the crossing track, while the front cars
start down the siding that will bring them alongside the mill
pond. This minor trespass upon the national rail network sub-
jected the locomotives to regular Interstate Commerce Commission inspections.

It's a later year and April's rains have come. The mill is no longer active, and the drying yard has been converted to parking spaces that await the season's visitors.

ALONG THE LEATHERBARK
—the shops and service area.

THE TRACKS CURVE left and we leave the mill area. Here is the railroad servicing area, itself vital to the logging operation. The water tank on the right side of the train and the coaling facilities on the left have the size and style more typical of a prosperous short line railroad than of a logging road. Those facilties do in fact result from a rail operation more substantial than the usually modest needs of a lumber railroad.

By the time West Virginia Spruce Lumber Company was absorbed into the pulp company, their Greenbrier & Elk River Railroad ran the eight miles up to the center of the woods operation. That spot was quite fittingly named Spruce and the railroad was franchised to carry passengers and freight up there. While it wasn't particularly rare to find a logging railroad chartered as a common carrier, most logging roads were not. The temporary trackage in the woods, used exclusively for logging, amounted to another thirty miles of line.

The grand scale on which the West Virginia Pulp & Paper Company thought and acted was now to be reflected in their railroad. A revised charter was obtained, giving the line a new name: the Greenbrier, Cheat & Elk Railroad. Two lengthy extensions were then built.

The western extension opened vast timberlands by crossing the crest of Cheat Mountain through an extremely deep cut. The northern extension connected with the Western Maryland Railway's branch from Elkins to Durbin. That extension not only provided coal mining opportunities but also safeguarded rail access to the timbering area by establishing an alternate route.

Seven years in the making, these extensions penetrated some of the Appalachian's highest and most rugged country. They added 74 miles of mainline to a railroad whose length, temporary tracks included, would later peak at 175 miles — the most anywhere for a logging railroad.

Not surprisingly, the railroad shops at Cass were substantial in size and capability. The modern buildings seen today replace shops destroyed by fire in 1972. The old shops sprawled along Leatherbark Creek's bottom-land, covering enough space to lay out five football fields. It was here, this place, that kept the mills, mines, and railroad running. There was little that couldn't be cast, machined, or built by the shopmen.

The logging industry had three distinct locomotive designs available for its special needs. These designs were essential where grades were steep, curves tight, roadbed rough, and alignment poor. All three designs featured gear drives to transmit power to the driving wheels. Only the Shay design was used at Cass in logging days, but an example of each of the other two has been brought here for historic comparison.

The Shay design is characterized by all steam cylinders being vertically positioned on the righthand side, just forward of the cab. This positioning causes the boiler to be offset to the left, giving a unique, asymmetrical appearance. Power is transmitted by a jointed drive shaft running the full length of the engine and tender with bevel gears at every wheel.

Over the years, the railroad owned thirteen Shays. Most were light engines to work the woods, but heavy duty service on the mainline into Spruce and Cass required large and powerful locomotives. Most remarkable was number 12. That giant was built in 1921 and proved so successful that the huge Cass shops were able to take further advantage of its design and rebuild it into the world's largest, heaviest, and most powerful Shay ever. Not bad going for a little place in the hills!

The familiar mists of morning begin to part. With a brakeman to grab a ride on the front step, reliable old No. 4 works the steep siding where fuel deliveries for the engines are made. An empty log car is being used to push a hopper car into its position on the wooden coaling trestle.

Always work safely — *to-day, to-night,* and *to-morrow.* **The old Victorian spellings have persisted here, but no matter, for even Franklin D. Roosevelt spelled that way and was easily understood. The crew seems to be in a contemplative mood. Small wonder, for it's August of 1960 and the logging era that started here back in Victorian days has just come to an end.**

[RIGHT:] The same engine is found in the same place as in the picture on the opposite page. But these are happier days because the threat of abandonment has been dispelled. All of Cass has a new purpose as two crewmen sweep the cinderfall from an open tourist car.

[BELOW:] Oil-burning No. 3 is being refueled by gravity from the Pennzoil tanker on the high track. As soon as proper air and fuel adjustments are made, that glorious plume of smoke will subside.

No day's work on the mountain starts without a full load of fuel. Soft coal is delivered in hopper cars that are pushed up onto the track on top of the wooden coal trestle. The coal is then emptied down into the coal pockets at the delivery deck where it is held until needed. The tenders of logging engines held only a few tons of coal, so loading does not take long, particularly when everybody lends a hand. A motor-driven coal conveyor is seen in the top picture, but the way it was really done is found at the center of the delivery deck. The fireman loads the tender a wheelbarrow at a time — and loads the wheelbarrow, a shovelful at a time. In the picture at the top right, there's lots of help! A scoopful or two from each of the shovelers and it's time for the other fellow to manhandle that little one-wheeled monster once more. A ground level view of No. 6 [BELOW, RIGHT] catches another wheelbarrow load going in.

Richard Carter

Elmer Burruss, Jr.

[OPPOSITE PAGE, TOP:] **It's May of 1972 and Shay No. 3 has just been completely refitted for service. After thirty years of duty in the forests of the Pacific Northwest, this engine was preserved at Portland, Oregon before being brought to Cass. But less than three months later, No. 3 was in the shops for a minor adjustment when the buildings were totally destroyed by fire. Another Shay and two flat cars were used to ram the shop doors, couple up, and pull her to safety. That heroic moment is captured in the lower left picture. Operations continued uninterrupted amid the ruins** [LOWER RIGHT], **until the new shop complex was completed in 1975,** [THIS PAGE, TOP].

[RIGHT:] **A regular chore for a Shay engineman is to lubricate the beveled driving gears. The circular member with the bolts in the lower left corner of the picture is one of the universal joints, a feature which permitted Shays to run well over poorly-laid track and around sharp curves.**

[LEFT:] **Before** dogging down No. 4's circular smokebox door, the shopman applies high-temperature sealing compound to get a good, tight seal. This view is inside the old shops.

[BELOW:] **Some** days are worse than others. No. 1 has derailed just as she started to back up out of the lower switchback. The maintenance-of-way speeder, also numbered 1, has arrived from Cass and the GMC truck with flanged wheels has come down from the mountain top, so there's plenty of help. The job will be more aggravating than difficult, for it's just a matter of jacking and judiciously using the re-railing irons.

[OPPOSITE PAGE:] **Here's** a good picture of the lower switchback track arrangements. No. 7 leads a double-headed train up from Cass and will continue up the stub track that's to the right and in back of the camera. Then, after the switch located just to the right of the picture has been thrown, the train will back up the track that curves steeply upward in the center of the photograph.

ON CHEAT MOUNTAIN
—touring the logging rails.

OUR TRAIN JOGS out of the shop area. We dodge along the waters of Leatherbark Creek, cross Back Mountain Road, and climb along the watercourse. In just two miles, we'll gain four hundred feet in altitude, a remarkable climb by the standards of an ordinary railroad. But, to the Shay and her crew, the push thus far is only so much fussing around.

At the two mile mark, the crevice between Cheat Mountain on the left and Back Mountain on the right becomes too pinched and too steep for any locomotive to maintain traction. We'll leave that narrow defile to the falling waters of the Leatherbark and, since there's no way to turn, we'll back up and around the face of the mountain.

This is the first of two switchbacks. A switchback is the last resort in mountain railroading. The process is to proceed past a trailing switch and then continue the journey by backing up, as if onto a siding. Actually, the siding is a continuation of the line itself. The reverse movements involved are time-consuming and ill-suited to heavy traffic.

Rugged as it is, the contour of the land pretty much dictates the location of the roadbed. Logging railroads generally didn't spend much money to avoid curves and steep grades. As a result, the cut-and-fill work and longer but gentler routes of standard railroad practice are usually dispensed with.

Another switchback, and then comes the famous 11 percent grade. There's a spot near Bald Knob that's steeper, but there is no instant more thrilling than the one which reveals the valley below. The deafening, frantic cacophony of smoke and steam subsides, for we have reached Whittaker Station.

Some trips end here, others go on to the very top. This point is not historically important, but its view, the experience of getting here, and the suitability for picnicking have led to its present day development.

The logging camps were farther up the mountain. Since the distance involved would have required valuable waking hours to commute, lumberjacks lived in the woods. It was rarely otherwise in the logging industry, so camp buildings or camp cars were an expected way of life for them. At the peak of activity, there were as many as fifteen camps. Typically, each camp had about 85 men, not the least important of which were the cook and his two or three helpers.

Work crews were assigned to clearing the limbs, topping and felling the trees, bucking the trunks into logs, skidding them to the nearest rail spur, and loading them onto cars. In early operations, horses were used for skidding the logs from the woods. At Cass, the need for teamsters and their horses was eliminated in 1919 by the use of three steam skidders. The new method was a substantial economy that improved overall productivity, but steam skidding left mountainside scars that have not yet disappeared. Perhaps they never will.

Follow-up crews cut smaller trees still standing and gathered slashings left by the loggers. This operation brought in the pulpwood, ready to have its bark removed. A pulp-peeling mill was built high on the mountain and thus, with the surrounding buildings, the town of Spruce was established. At 3853 feet above sea level, this was the highest town in the eastern United States.

In addition to the lumber and pulp activities, the totally integrated operation included five coal mines, an extraction plant to obtain wood chemicals, company stores, farms, and of course, the railroad.

The peak years of this empire were the Teens and Twenties. Ultimately, the supply of timber

[ABOVE:] **There's still a bit of a misty mood at Cass this working day. Other shifting chores done, No. 4 eases up to a string of empties under the watchful eye of the brakeman. After coupling onto the logging flats, it will be up onto Cheat Mountain one more time. The flat cars were basic transportation only, riding on simple arch-bar trucks and having truss rods to keep their wooden frames leveled up.** [RIGHT:] **Barely out of the shop area, the empties go log-hunting. Thrust mountainward along the Leatherbark, they cross Back Mountain Road. The next stop: the lower switchback.**

Between switchbacks, the engineer leans out backwards in the direction of travel, away from the camera. Six cars back, the brakemen trail by taking in the sights. Yes, it's almost heaven — a perfect place seen in the perfect way.

Through the second switchback, the engine again pushes. This is mountain railroading, uphill style. At this steep section, the track rises a man's height in just two car lengths, enough to affect the behavior of the water level in the boiler. As if that weren't enough of a concern for the fireman, the turbid blast from the stack produces a draft across the fire so strong that the fire looks ready to jump right off the grates. But just for a few moments, the point we know as Whittaker is getting close.

that could be harvested on the grand scale became exhausted. The two railroad branches that had been built out of Spruce were sold in 1927 to the Western Maryland Railway. Their interest in the lines related to mineral deposits, not logging. In 1939, the mill at Spruce was closed and by 1942, West Virginia Pulp & Paper had disposed of their holdings at Cass.

In the generation and a half since the initial cutting had been done on Cheat Mountain, a second growth of trees, mostly hardwoods, presented an opportunity for a smaller scale operation. The buyer was F. Edwin Mower of Charleston, West Virginia. During the Mower

Lumber Company years, operations were extended into previously marginal areas.

But time, turn-of-the-century methods and equipment, and an overhead inherited from the bonanza days, all worked against Mower. When he died, the time had come to call it quits. The mill and railroad closed down July 1, 1960.

Scrapping began. The skidders, loaders, and some other equipment were burned in order to recover the scrap metal. Track was being removed at the rate of a half a mile a day. And then the miracle happened, but that is the next part of our story.

Trees are where you find them, not where you wish they'd be. It was necessary to lay tracks into general areas of a tract in order to work the surrounding subdivisions. Being temporary, the trackage was built as cheaply as possible without jeopardizing the safety of men and equipment, yet strong enough to carry the payloads out. [LEFT:] A track gang elsewhere in West Virginia extends the logging rails. [BELOW:] The absence of ballast and sketchy alignment left mountain-top spur tracks with more wrinkles than a hungry belly.

[ABOVE:] **One mountain-top railroad activity was the re-location of the log loader to another place where logs have been dumped, waiting to be loaded. Moving the loader was not a rare operation, but pictures of the move, particularly from this angle in back of the cab, are.** [RIGHT:] **Another mountain-top maneuver is partially completed. The left-hand track is a dead end siding and the object is to get the cars in there without trapping the engine in front of them. So, the crew has uncoupled the engine, pulled it onto the righthand track, and thrown the track switch so that the cars can be towed onto the left track by means of a cable. Just like a mule pulling a barge on a canal.**

In the woods, there were various sets, as the temporary locations were called, where a steam skidder would be positioned. The elements at this set include the railvan that the skidder crew used to get back to camp, a carload of coal to fuel the skidder, the skidder itself numbered 1, the head spar, and in the center, the log loader sitting on a flat car. As loading progressed, a loader would move along the flat cars on small wheels that used the flat car side sills as guide rails. The log landing is to the side and in back of the loader. [LEFT:] Amid a welter of guy wires, a skidder crewman inspects the lead and trip blocks on the head spar.

Philip Ronfor

A sling full of logs skids into the landing area from the right, lead ends high. Known as high-lead skidding, the method replaced skidding the logs out of the forest by having teams of horses drag them. In a separate operation, the man on the log car is using a cant hook to handle the logs raised from the landing by the steam loader. Difficult work requiring strength and perserverance, logging is still one of the most dangerous major occupations.

Philip Ronfor

27

Philip Ronfor

Loading this flatcar has barely begun. This is the fourth log being guided into place on the deck of the car. About three dozen logs of this second growth hardwood will constitute a carload. The side poles are in place and after the load is made up, the safety chains will be dogged down so that the load is tightly gripped. [BELOW:] A loaded train moves out from another spot on the mountain and [OPPOSITE PAGE] four cars are on their way to the mill in a classic scene from the penultimate days of logging.

Livin' on top of the world describes this camp car set, but the reference is to height above sea level, not the opulence of rich living. Old-time loggers, content to live in isolation for extended periods of time and to work from dawn to dusk, were becoming scarce as better access to the woods made logging communities the home base for the men and their families. [ABOVE:] This was the last camp and, as was customary, foodstuffs were needed in the case load lot. [BELOW:] A few stalwarts unload the staples.

Philip Ronfor

30

Resourcefulness was one of the attributes needed to keep machinery running up on top of the mountain. [RIGHT:] A regular spot was provided for care and adjustments to the engine. The engineer stands on a plank walk to set matters straight. [ABOVE:] Cinders have clogged the screen on the smokestack. Brute force in the form of a brake club is applied to whack things clear but, as things sometimes ended up, it was necessary to handle the hot, grimy screen in order to get to the root of a problem.

Whether logs or tourists, the watchword on the descent is control. Speed is the enemy. Operating the locomotive on the downhill end of the train provided a plus for safety in case of coupling failure. In tourist service, this practice has the added advantage of helping to keep the shower of cinders from landing on the passengers.

Arrival at Whittaker is heralded by the pole-type welcoming archway seen at the rear. Passengers usually stroll about taking in the air and scenery, perhaps enjoying a bite or two at a picnic table.

The Gum family owned and worked the land before there was a Cass. Harry grew up in the shadow of Cheat Mountain and spanned the eras from pulpwood to hardwood to tourist days. Vast, but undeveloped, caverns lie beneath these ancestral hills. A Cass Scenic Railroad trip rounds the knoll overlooking the farm. |LEFT:| The cattle seem better adjusted to the presence of trains than to the presence of photographers.

HARRY P. GUM FARM

[ABOVE:] **The climb continues. At the first scenic overlook beyond Whittaker, the rails cling to the side of the hill. Wooden ties are used as cribbing to retain the roadbed where it needed building out a bit.**

[OPPOSITE PAGE, TOP:] **This was Spruce. The powerhouse and pulp peeling mill are in the foreground, houses and dormitories in the left background. Seen here in 1914, abandonment was still a quarter century away. Bald Knob passengers look out over this high, cold, and now deserted site as their train passes the 4200 foot elevation.** [OPPOSITE PAGE, MIDDLE:] **Before 1972, Bald Knob trains passed under the arch and entered a steep S-curve that required double-heading when trains were longer than four cars. The grading in the foreground is for a line relocation that both straightened the approach and reduced the grade.** [OPPOSITE, BOTTOM:] **No question about it, this is West Virginia! Bald Knob's pavilion commands a view of the valley and the tumultuous sea of mountains beyond. Only Spruce Knob, a couple of dozen miles to the north, is higher and because of the altitude, both experience temperature ranges typical of the softwood areas of Canada.**

PRESERVATION
—a unique attraction.

THERE REALLY WASN'T much basis for hoping that Cass would be revived, or so it seemed in 1960. Apparently the life cycle of a logging town had run its course and reached the bitter end. From the viewpoint of lumbering, that was of course true — and that *was* the conventional viewpoint.

It was the unconventional viewpoint that saved the day. That view came first from Russell Baum, a logging railfan. Curiously, this man's name could not have been more appropriate: *baum* is the German word for tree!

In coming to Cass again, just to see things one more time, he realized that others also had asked Mower Lumber for permission to look around and ride with the crew. Perhaps there were many people who would like the chance to mix some scenery and excitement with a look at an important West Virginia industry.

We know today that the idea was a great one. At the time, the crucial need was an effective action plan that would mobilize enough resources to do the job of saving Cass. This was done by aiming for state-wide support and detail planning by a commission that would merit the attention and approval of the state legislature.

For all those who participated in the mission, July 10, 1962 was the culmination of their remarkable effort: the state had purchased the property and equipment that would be needed.

The first tourist run was on June 15, 1963, just five days before the state's 100th birthday. Public response was sensational from the start, a tribute to the foresight of all who made it happen.

As expected, the property needed extensive rehabilitation, for only a few years earlier, things were headed for the scrap pile. The line to Bald Knob was built and logging equipment was replaced as part of the restoration plan. Of course, more remains to be done in due time in order to completely recapture logging days.

Most interesting from the railroading aspect were the additional locomotives that were brought to Cass. Several Shays were obtained to protect the operating schedule, and examples of both other geared locomotive designs were also acquired. Those designs, the Heisler and the Climax, were driven by a line shaft that ran underneath the engine on the centerline, instead of along the side as with the Shays. Heisler and Climax differed, however, on the placement and connection of their steam cylinders.

The developmental plan had been augmented by an imaginative operating plan. Charters have always been possible and the following photographs illustrate the range of activites that preservation has made possible. It does indeed help us to get a feel for this part of West Virginia's history. That's just the way Kyle Neighbors wanted it to be.

Triple-headed action was called for on Dedication Day. Governor Barron, his aides, and the press have just been treated to a smoky spectacular between the switchbacks. After all that heavy steaming, the Shays did not have sufficient water reserve to lay over on the mountain while ceremonies took place. Like lumberjacks, they seem to drink their own weight in less time than it takes to get to the woods. [LEFT:] Two of the Shays scamper back to Cass for water.

To assure that Cass Scenic would have adequate motive power, Shay No. 7 was bought from the Meadow River Lumber Company at Rainelle. Before sending the engine over to Cass under her own power, she was refurbished and had Cass lettering applied. The big baloon stack, a Radley-Hunter design, was particularly effective when wood was used for fuel. This view catches the delivery move on C&O tracks at Sandstone, 21 miles from her old home with 129 more to go before reaching Cass. [BELOW:] There couldn't be a better place for a young railfan to watch what's going on than from the back platform of a wooden caboose. This is Shay No. 3's first day of service and adjustments are still being made before starting up the hill.

[ABOVE:] Not all chartered trains are passenger runs to the mountain. In this instance, a Heisler locomotive, rack-type log cars, a log loader, and caboose were used to re-create a once-familiar West Virginia scene. At Cass, historical and educational opportunities take many forms.
[RIGHT:] The Lima Locomotive Works built Shays. In 1927, they improved the product line with a larger, more powerful design that was primarily intended for western operations. Termed the Pacific Coast Shay, the model featured all-weather cabs, oil firing, and many engineering improvements. This is a fitting addition to the Cass locomotive roster, for she's the only Pacific Coast model to ever operate in the East.

[TOP:] A railfan double-header stops to draw water from a trackside tank located below the planking. Next comes the 13% grade, steepest on the line and beyond that, Bald Knob. [ABOVE:] Railroad portraiture at night is a particularly dramatic art form. Multiple flash exposures are used and care is taken to highlight surroundings as well as the train itself.